ART AND HISTORY OF
HAIFA

AKKO-CAESAREA-BEIT SHEARIM
DALIYAT-EL-KARMEL

BONECHI & STEIMATZKY

Welcome to Haifa!
You have come to the most beautiful city in Israel and probably
in the Mediterranean basin. A city which combines stunning natural beauty
with the amenities of a big city.
Whether you stroll along scenic Panorama street on the ridge of Mount Carmel,
or stretch your muscles jogging on the silky shores
along the clear blue waters of the sea,
the breathtaking views of Haifa are with you all the time.
Our city's history spans a period from
the pre-historic cave man of Mount Carmel,
through Biblical Shikmona and the walled in City dating back
to the Ottoman Empire, to Haifa of the 20th century.
Rare relics of these periods are displayed inHaifa's numerous museums.
We also take great pride in the peaceful coexistence in the City between
Jews, Moslems and Christians. The Bahaian faith has chosen Haifa
as its center,and its shrines are masterpieces of architecture and gardening
and should certainly be visited.
Haifa is an ideal base for visits to Northern Israel.
You are within an hour or two hours
drive to the picturesque Druze villages on Mount Carmel, Nazareth,
the Sea of Galilee, the Golan Heights and Mount Hermon.
We are planning to make Haifa even more attractive to tourists.
In various stages of development are: a marina, an exhibition and fairs center,
new modern hotels along the seafront, restaurants, cafés and night clubs,
and a major face lifting for the old parts of the City, including
the German Colony founded by the Templars over one hundred years ago.
I sincerely hope that you will enjoy your stay in Haifa,
and that this is just the first of many more visits to our fair city.
In conclusion I wish to express my appreciation
and thanks to Steimatzky,publishers of this guide,
for making a visit to Haifa a more enlightening one.

Major General (Ret.)
AMRAM MITZNA
Mayor of Haifa

The glowing panorama of Haifa at night.

HAIFA

Third largest city in Israel in terms of population, Haifa is the country's foremost seaport and an emerging industrial, business, research and cultural center. But to think of Haifa as an essentially modern city, made dreary by industrialization and substantially barren from the point of view of landscape and natural attractions, is a mistake. The city, arising on the lush green slopes of Mount Carmel, overlooking its crescent bay (*Mifraz Hefa*) and extending north to Akko point, is instead a verdant urban center abounding in luxuriant parks and gardens, built on three distinct levels. From the primitive coastal settlement of *Shiqmona*, the *Sycaminum* of old, a Phoenician center for the production of purple dyes well-known to Pythagoras and to the Romans, to the city's oldest residential quarter, *Hadar*, at the foot of Mount Carmel, home to today's high-technology industries and a center of business and commerce, all the way up to *Carmel Center*, in its panoramic setting on the very crest of the mountain and with its sumptuous villas, splendid private homes and luxury hotels,

Haifa's streets, dotted with characteristic sidewalk cafés and restaurants featuring international cuisine, are a standing invitation to go for a stroll - and your walk may well lengthen into a true outing along the well-marked trails of **Mount Carmel National Park**.

Although Haifa's name derives in equal measure from the name Caiaphas, its presumed founder, and from the Hebrew expression *Yafe* (meaning 'beautiful beach'), we know that its safe port was renowned as early as the 2nd Century B.C. The city later became a Crusader stronghold, although it was a long time eclipsed by the nearby Saint John of Acre (*Akko*). Haifa blossomed again only when Akko fell into decline and thanks to major railway construction in the 19th and 20th centuries. Today the 'City of the Future', as T. Herzl, founder of the Zionist movement, defined it, Haifa is an active center with longstanding labourist traditions (in fact, it is sometimes called the 'Red City'). As a popular saying goes, "in Haifa you work, in Tel Aviv you play, and in Jerusalem you pray".

Haifa, Carmel Center: these prospects document the modern image of one of the city's greenest and most dynamic residential neighborhoods, with its skyline marked by the soaring outlines of skyscrapers and hotel buildings.

MOUNT CARMEL

"Your head is held high like Mount Carmel and your hair is like the purple": thus wrote the poet-king Solomon in the *Song of Songs*, ten centuries before Christ. Although this is surely the first written mention of Haifa's outstanding mountain, fact and legend would have it that Mount Carmel was the dwelling-place of the Prophet Elijah, Pythagoras' spiritual retreat, and probably also a shelter for the Holy Family. Saint Louis stopped there in Medieval times, and, relatively more recently, so did Napoleon, William II and the painter Chagall.

The first enclaves in prehistoric times would seem to date back to Neanderthal man. The name of the mountain derives from the Hebrew expression *Kerem-El*, meaning 'God's vineyard'. What is certain is that this impressive peak, softened by abundant greenery, shaded by the canopies of the cluster pines and ennobled by the gracious profiles of the

Haifa, shops along a Carmel Center boulevard.

Haifa, panoramic walks through the lush greenery of the Mount Carmel gardens. At the bottom an Ottoman cannon and the 1948 War Memorial.

cypress trees, is a sort of natural paradise, and every effort is being made to preserve the environmental and naturalistic heritage of the territory (2000 of the 21,600 acres of the national park have been set aside as nature reserve). Gazelles and deer roam free in this vast expanse of wild land, with its marked hiking trails and rest and picnic areas. The Carmel Range (*Har Karmel*) extends 25 kilometers from northwest to southwest and is followed by the Kishon River as it runs toward the Yezreel Valley. Mount Carmel's residential neighborhoods are known for their modern, full-comfort accommodations, the shopping districts, and the pleasant, relaxing promenades and trails that wind through an incomparably panoramic natural setting.

MANE KATZ MUSEUM

Almost at the top of Mount Carmel, with a splendid view of the bay, the house where the famous painter Mane Katz lived the last four years of his life now houses the Museum that bears his name.

Born in Ukraine in 1894, Emmanuel Katz was one of a group of artists who lived and worked in Paris in the years between World War I and II.

Color was the prime means of expression for Mane Katz, rather than form or composition. Shortly before the end he wrote: "Details are less important than the spirit of work, the atmosphere, the feelings".

The Museum, a white late 19th-century structure, is furnished with antiques and fine Persian carpets. The works exhibited alternate, chosen from the hundreds of oil paintings, drawings and sculptures the artist bequeathed to the city of Haifa when he died in 1962.

The Entrance to the Museum.

A view of some of the rooms.

Hommage to Paris.

Interior of a Synagogue.

Three Rabbis.

Interior with Harmonium.

Haifa, two aspects of the Sculpture Garden, where Ursula Malbin's bronze sculptures contrast with the green of the panoramic gardens.

Haifa, two panoramic vistas toward the port. In the lower foreground the massive structure of the Dagon Grain Silo.

SCULPTURE GARDEN

The 'Sculpture Garden' is located in the *French Carmel* neighborhood, across the street from 135 *Zionism Avenue*.

This public space, one of the many parks and gardens set apart for relaxation and recreation that contribute to mellowing the image of a city as hardworking as it is hospitable, is one of the favorite stopping-places of connoisseurs of modern sculpture. In an inspiring scenographic setting, it hosts a score of works by the sculptress Ursula Malbin. The sculptures, marked by their sense of movement and the plasticity of the forms, create fascinating contrasts in bronze with the green of the plants and the trees, while in the background breathtaking panoramic vistas sweep from the city to the port and all its appurtenances and out over the intensely blue waters of the bay itself.

11

These suggestive images bear faithful witness to the beauty of the city of Haifa, agreeably spread out on the slopes of Mount Carmel overlooking the picturesque bay. The full panorama at the top of the page shows the mighty outline of the Dagon Grain Silo (on the left) and the golden dome of the Bahai Shrine (Shrine of the Báb), immersed in the green of the cypresses (on the right); at the center of the photograph, beyond the transparent blue of the sea waters, is the profile of the strip of land coming to a point at Akko, the ancient stronghold of Saint Jean d'Acre that closes off Haifa Bay to the northeast.
At the bottom of the page a prospect of the modern yet substantially 'green' city opening to the sea (on the left) and a detail of the beautiful dome of the Bahai Shrine (on the right).

Haifa, a glimpse of the Universal House of Justice.

Haifa, view of the luxuriant gardens surrounding the Bahai Shrine, also known as the 'Persian Gardens'.

Haifa, a picturesque prospective of the Bahai Shrine, crowned by its elegant golden dome.

BAHAI SHRINE AND GARDENS

Splendidly set in the charming green Mount Carmel landscape with its extensive reaches of maquis, cypresses and cluster pines, the Bahai complex includes the *Mausoleum of the Báb* and two buildings in strongly Neoclassical style: the *International Archives* and the *Universal House of Justice*, from which the spiritual affairs of the International Bahai Community are administered. The marvelously luxuriant *Gardens* open out all around. The splendid golden dome of the mausoleum marks the Mount Carmel landscape; the grand building, outstanding for the Oriental flavour of its architecture, is the resting-place of the mortal remains of the Báb, brought to Haifa from Tabriz in Persia in 1909.

In 1844, Siyyid Ali Muhammad, later to be known as Báb, or "The Gateway", foretold the coming of that Messenger of God so long awaited by the entire world, and placed himself at the service of mankind that men might prepare for the second coming. Thus was the Bahai Faith born. The professions of the Báb were immediately taken as a threat to the Moslem religion; the Báb was arrested and later publicly executed by a firing squad in Tabriz.

These images can suggest only a fraction of the scenographic beauty, the charm and the magical enchantment of the 'Persian Gardens' across Zionism Avenue from the Bahai Shrine. The choreographic feel of the floral and ornamental motifs, recalling every now and then the patterns of the Persian carpets and the well-chosen setting in the landscape make these gardens one of the most sought-out destinations of tourists seeking simple relaxation amidst the green of the lush vegetation and the color of a full spectrum of bright-hued blossoms.
Particularly memorable are the attractive artistic wrought-iron railings and the marble sepulchral monuments, resembling small temples, containing the mortal remains of Bahaullah's close relatives.

Following his execution, a wave of violence broke over his followers, among whom a certain Husayn Ali, member of a noble family descending from an imperial dynasty that had reigned in ancient Persia, who publicly avowed the teachings of the Báb and offered protection to his persecuted brethren. Deprived of his privileges and his worldly goods, he was tortured, imprisoned and condemned to exile. And it was from that very internment in Baghdad that in 1863 he proclaimed himself he whose coming the Báb had foretold and became Bahaullah, the "Glory of God", founder of the Bahai Faith: a religious movement with no clergy, whose central creed is the unification of mankind in a great family and in a common homeland. From Baghdad to Constantinople and then to Adrianople; thus in 1868 did Bahaullah reach the Holy Land. He was held as prisoner of the Turkish government in the Citadel of Akko until he was allowed to move to Bahjí, in the environs the city, where he died in 1892 and where his mortal remains still rest.

CARMELITE MONASTERY

Also known as *Stella Maris*, the interesting group of religious buildings, including the beautiful Basilica and one of what are called Elijah's Caves, arises on that part of Mount Carmel that becomes a promontory jutting out over the transparent Mediterranean blue waters of Haifa Bay.

It would seem that on this site, one of the loveliest belvederes of the city, there stood as early as the second half of the 6th century a monastery taking its name from Elijah. Fallen into ruin, it was retaken during the Crusades by the Knights Templars; the convent of Saint Margaret of the Carmelites, probably the reconstruction and enlargement of an earlier Greek Orthodox center, also stood there in later times. Tradition has it that in the 12th Century a small band of Crusaders settled in solitary retreat on the Carmel promontory, founding a community in

Haifa, two aspects of the exterior of the Stella Maris Carmelite Monastery complex.

Stella Maris, a detail of the Madonna of the Carmel, a gift from Chile.

Stella Maris, a view of the interior of the Basilica with the entry to Elijah's Cave.

Stella Maris, the interior of the cupola, with frescoes depicting episodes from the lives of Elijah and Elisha.

Stella Maris, the high altar of the Basilica, with the statue of the Madonna of the Carmel.

which asceticism and prayer were a way of life, in the very places that had offered shelter to the Biblical Prophets Elijah and Elisha.

At the beginning of the 13th Century, Alberto da Vercelli, Latin Patriarch of Jerusalem, codified the Carmelite rule; after moving to Europe the Carmelites followed the model of the mendicant orders.

The present-day **Carmelite Monastery** is a late-19th Century reconstruction of a pre-existing building razed to the ground in 1891 by Abdullah Pacha, who used the site as a quarry for materials for building his private residence.

The **Basilica** also dates to the 19th Century; it is a church in the form of a Greek cross, crowned by a dome. Of note the use of precious marbles to face the interior walls. The sumptuous high altar is adorned by a sculpture, in Cedar of Lebanon, of the *Madonna of the Carmel*. The frescoed interior of the

Stella Maris, two views of the grotto known as Elijah's Cave.

dome depicts *episodes from the lives of the Prophets Elijah and Elisha*.

Elijah's Cave, as it is called, opens under the chancel of the Basilica. The entry is flanked by two porphyry columns. The evocative interior contains the altar, placed against a rock ledge which would seem to have been the hermit's pallet. Remains uncovered during excavations suggest that the cave was also used as a burial-place over the centuries. Whatever the truth may be, this site is directly associated with the Prophet's sojourn in the area. It appears that Elijah was active in the north Kingdom of Israel during the first half of the 10th Century B.C; a firm believer in monotheism, he challenged the priests of Baal on Mount Carmel and later also Jezebel, wife of Achab, who had spoken in their favor.

According to traditional iconography, the Prophet was seen ascending to Heaven in a flaming chariot by his disciple Elisha.

21

Haifa, the modern panoramic cableway system linking the seaside boulevards and Stella Maris.

Haifa, the Naval Maritime Museum from above.

Haifa, panoramic vista from the Stella Maris terrace.

STELLA MARIS CABLEWAY

The modern cableway system is a delightful alternative to the automobile for reaching the Stella Maris Carmelite Monastery. The attractive, comfortable cabins leave from the station at the foot of the mountain near the seafront promenade and ascend the slope to French Carmel. The less hurried tourist should try this means of transport, if for no reason other than to experience the pleasant thrill of the aerial journey and the privilege of savoring to the fullest the incomparable natural beauty of Mount Carmel and of drinking in unparalleled panoramic vistas of the city and its bay.

NAVAL MARITIME MUSEUM

The collections belonging to this museum, founded near the end of the 1970s, are housed in a building in contemporary style. The exhibits offer an interesting perspective on the design and construction of model ships and the history of navigation in the Mediterranean basin, the Red Sea and the Indian Ocean from 20 centuries before Christ through the end of the 17th Century A.D.

Haifa, a perspective of the colossal Dagon Grain Silo, home to the Dagon Grain Museum.

Haifa, two views of Elijah's second Cave, also known as the 'School of the Prophets'.

Following pages: *Haifa, two splendid nighttime images of the Bahai Shrine.*

DAGON GRAIN MUSEUM

The exhibits in this quite singular museum collection are housed in the **Dagon Grain Silo** in the immediate vicinity of the port. The silo, built midway through the 1950s, was for a long time the highest building in Haifa. Its impressive silhouette is still today a distinctive feature of the cityscape and is visible from a great distance. Quite probably this is the only grain silo in the world to have any architectural pretensions; the style of the building, in fact, manifestly complies to the tenets typical of the Oriental schools of architecture.

The *Archaeological Museum of Grain Storage and Handling in Israel* provides an interesting overview of the history of how the precious cereal has been preserved and distributed in the country, from the most remote times to the present. The collection contains ceramics, old agricultural tools, coins and reconstructions of ancient silos in Israel and the Near East, as well as a model illustrating how the Dagon silo system operates today.

ELIJAH'S CAVE

This natural cave, accessible through a garden at the base of the Carmel promontory, has a very long history. It is thought to have been a place of meditation and worship since the very dawn of civilization. If on the one hand the cave is also known as the *School of the Prophets*, in deference to the tradition that associates the cave with Elijah and his lessons to his disciples (9th Century B.C.), on the other it is also believed to have been the retreat chosen by the philosopher Pythagoras for his meditations. The Roman Emperor Vespasiano was another of the cave's illustrious visitors. Christian tradition has renamed it the *Grotto of the Madonna*, evidently with reference to the Holy Family's stopover on their return from Egypt. It was certainly the retreat of those hermits who in the 12th Century founded the Carmelite Order on Mount Carmel. An interesting and eloquent mention of the site is found in Islamic tradition as well: for the Muslims, the cave is in fact the *Grotto of el-Khadar*.

UNIVERSITY

Just outside the built-up area, on the summit of Mount Carmel in a panoramic park setting, rise the buildings of the University of Haifa, which serves the entire northern portion of the country. The University, founded at the beginning of the 1970s, is dominated by the soaring the **Eshkol Tower**, a mighty creation by the Brazilian architect Oscar Niemeyer. From its top, visibility permitting, one can enjoy a view as fascinating as it is sweeping. Among the city's scientific institutions we must also mention the **Technion** (Israel's Institute of Technology), home to the interesting **Museum of Science and Technology.**

Mount Carmel (Haifa), the University's Eshkol Tower, rising above the profile of the verdant hills.

Daliyat-el-Karmel, typical products of Druze craftsmanship.

DALIYAT-EL-KARMEL

This quaint village is reached by the road that runs through *Mount Carmel National Park*. The locality, once known as *Daliyat-el-Druze*, is unusual in that all its inhabitants are members of a Druze community.

The Druze are an ethnic-religious community of Islamic derivation and are concentrated mainly in Lebanon and in Syria, although certain minorities also live in Israel and in Jordan. Their religion derives from the Ishmaelitish faith and originated in Egypt at the turn of the 10th-11th centuries.

The picturesque hamlet, known for the traditional hospitality of its people, stands out in its well-chosen setting in the natural landscape of hills and valleys that spreads out to the southeast of Haifa. Ancient archaeological finds have been uncovered nearby. The typical local costumes and the ancient customs attract visitors to the colorful **Bazaar** where local handcrafts are sold.

Daliyat-el-Karmel, an elder of the Druze community; a Druze woman intent on making bread.

Saint John of Acre, a detail of the walls.

Saint John of Acre, an aerial view of the port.

Saint John of Acre, a view of the seawalls.

AKKO
(SAINT JOHN OF ACRE)

In a splendid position on the promontory that marks the northern limit of Haifa's picturesque bay stands the ancient city of **Akko**, with its oldest enclave still enclosed by the original circle of walls. Beyond the city walls lie the more recently developed areas. The beauty of Akko's natural setting will astonish the visitor and hold him spellbound whether he arrives by sea or is fortunate enough to be able to admire the city from above as he flies over it. The architectural style, the ages-old quality of the buildings and the stone walls, the domes of the mosques and the slim, soaring minarets combine to give Akko the air of a genuinely Levantine city.

A Phoenician colony dating to very ancient times, Akko was first mentioned in the Tel Amarna Tablets and later in the annals of Pharaoh Thutmoses III. Named *Aka* by the Greeks, the city was rebuilt in the 3rd century B.C. by Ptolemy II Philadelphus, who renamed it *Ptolemais*; the Arab conquest again changed the city's name (to *Akka*). Finally, during the Crusades (12th Century), when the military stronghold was entrusted to the keeping of the Knights of the Hospitaller Order of St. John, the city was given the name by which it is still known today: *Saint Jean d'Acre* (Saint John of Acre). It was soon to become the capital of the Eastern Latin Kingdom and a well-known commercial center on the routes sailed by the fleets of the Italian Maritime Republics and the Provençal merchants, but was razed to the ground after the Mameluke conquest (1292), to rise again only about the middle of the 18th Century thanks to the work of Sheiks Dahir-el-Omar and his successor Ahmed el Jazzar (nicknamed 'the Butcher' due to his ferocity, but redeemed by his excellence as a town planner). In the Napoleonic period a second circle of walls was raised around Saint John of Acre; for a brief period during the 19th Century the city fell under Egyptian control. The slow decline of the city, to the advantage of nearby Haifa, began when the port later silted up.

Saint John of Acre, these images illustrate different aspects of the Citadel, erected by order of Ahmed el Jazzar on the ruins of the old Crusader city.
The Citadel, here in its entirety, a turret seen from the enclosed courtyard, and some interior spaces distinguished by their typical cross-vaults, was used over the course of time as an arsenal and as a prison. Particularly memorable episodes include the detention of Bahaullah and the merciless executions of the Hebrew nationalists during the British mandate in Palestine.

Bahjí, not far from Akko, is the holy place most venerated by the followers of the Bahai Faith, who from all around the world come there as pilgrims to pray at the *Mausoleum of the Báb*. The splendid *Gardens* which frame the temple are a favorite stopping place for thousands of visitors. Adjacent to the mausoleum is the *House* in which the founder of the Bahai Faith spent his last years, a life-long political prisoner, and died in 1892.

CITADEL

The massive structure of the Citadel of Saint John of Acre is without doubt one of the most outstanding monuments of the city. With its heavy stone walls, which arise on the site of what was once the Crusader city, it is among the most distinctive features of the cityscape.

The Citadel was built on the ancient Crusader ruins under Ahmed el Jazzar (18th Century); the new building's original function was that of military headquarters for the city's rulers. It was later to become the arsenal, and then a prison when the city fell under Turkish rule. The long detention of Bahaullah (Husayn Ali), the founder of the Bahai Faith dates to this period (second half of the 19th century). The central portion of the Citadel is topped by the **Treasure Tower**, so named after the spoils of pillages accumulated there by El Jazzar. During the British mandate in Palestine (beginning in 1922), the English transformed this portion of the fortress into a prison; many activists of the Hebrew nationalist movement were confined there. In 1947 a raid, as spectacular as it was reckless, by Hebrew commandos allowed at least 200 prisoners to escape. The following year the soldiers of the new State of Israel broke Arab resistance, overpowering the garrison and taking the city.

Saint John of Acre, an evocative glimpse of the el Jazzar Mosque.

Saint John of Acre, this small temple, standing in the courtyard of the el Jazzar Mosque, is the burial place of the Mosque's founder.

Saint John of Acre, the stairway leading up to the el Jazzar Mosque.

EL JAZZAR MOSQUE

This largest of the seven mosques standing in Akko is without doubt also the most beautiful and the most impressive. Its characteristic architectural lines, clearly reflecting those of Islamic and Oriental art, make it one of the finest examples of religious architecture in the entire country; nor must we forget that it is also the largest mosque in Israel. Construction was completed in 1781 by Ahmed el Jazzar, whose tomb is situated in the courtyard of the building in a small temple with a colonnade and a cupola. For building his Mosque, Ahmed el Jazzar ordered use of special construction materials subtracted specifically for that purpose from important archaeological sites including Caesarea and Tyre and shipped to Akko. The courtyard adds emphasis to the splendid proportions of the central part of the Mosque building, with its open arcade of ogival arches standing before the facade as such, which is embellished with geometric marble decoration. The grandiose central

Saint John of Acre (el Jazzar Mosque), these views show the elegant pointed arches and small cupolas of the portico; a detail of the fabulous geometric decorations in polychrome marble; various aspects of the interior of the Islamic temple, memorable for the sumptuous preciosity of its decoration.

dome overhead is flanked by numerous smaller cupolas, and the dome or cupola motif is repeated over the three sides of the portico opening onto the courtyard. The spire of the minaret is the indispensable complement to the Mosque, even though the picturesque figure of the *Muezzin*, who five times each day climbed to its top to summon the faithful to prayer, has today been replaced by an impersonal tape-recorded voice over loudspeakers. Outside the building is the traditional *lustral font*, used by the Muslims for their ritual ablutions before entering the temple. In the interior of the Mosque, with its wonderful polychrome ceramic decorations, arabesques and marble facings, is the *Mihrab*, a niche facing in the direction of the Mecca to guide the faithful during prayers. The walls are adorned with epigraphs in Arabic script. The Mosque arises on the site of at least three earlier places of worship, both Christian and Islamic. Remains of Crusader structures have been discovered.

CRYPT OF THE KNIGHTS OF ST. JOHN

The history of the noble city of Akko is clearly traced in its monumental ruins; so much so that here, in an environment that has preserved much of the original appearance of the city intact since the 13th century, we can admire vestiges that have come down to us unaltered from the period of the Crusades. Among the numerous chambers making up the subterranean Crusader city (over which the Citadel was raised), one of which, the **Grand Maneir**, seat of Crusader administration, still shows traces of the works ordered by El Jazzar for building his Citadel, the suggestive Crypt of the Knights of St. John is especially memorable. Once the refectory and meeting hall of the rulers of England and France, the room stands out for the grandeur of the massive pillars supporting splendid Gothic ribbed cross-vaults. Of note the *fleur-de-lis of France* sculpted in the rock: a singular union of the emblem of the Catholic kings and a motif of that most traditional of Islamic iconographies which, prevented from depicting the human form, left a great profusion of floral and geometric decoration.

Saint John of Acre, some highly evocative images of the suggestive Crypt of the Knights of Saint John, set apart by its impressive pillars and its vaulted ceiling with ribbed transepts.

40

THE HISTORICAL CITY CENTER

The atmosphere of the oldest section of Saint John of Acre is fascinating, and tempting for the tourist who would make of the area his own 'personal discovery', wandering through the picturesque narrow streets and alleys where the dominant element is stone - in the pavements of the streets and in the houses that face onto them. All through the ancient *Souk*, the **Turkish Market**, also known as the *White Market*, the shops opening one after the other onto the narrow passage through their beautiful ogival arches are an enchanting sight. There is something for everyone among the many goods displayed in this market, founded, as tradition would have it, by Dahar el Omar in the mid-18th Century (and renovated in the 1800s). Barely time for a glimpse at the domes and the minaret of the **El Zeituna Mosque**, and our eye is caught by an ancient **Turkish Bathhouse** (*Hamman el Basha*), now the **Municipal Museum** and home to collections of archaeological and folkloristic documentation as well as a collection of antique weapons.

Saint John of Acre, a corner of the colorful Souk (Turkish covered market).

Saint John of Acre, a prospect of the El Zeituna Mosque.

Saint John of Acre, a characteristic alleyway in the picturesque historic city center.

Saint John of Acre, a room in the Municipal Museum now housed in the old Turkish Bathhouse.

Saint John of Acre, some glimpses down the alluring alleyways of the ancient Crusader center.

Saint John of Acre, a general view of the Caravansary of the Pillars, with the Clock Tower; and some details of the columned portico.

CARAVANSARY OF THE PILLARS

Known locally as *Khan el Umdan*, or 'Caravansary of the Pillars', this is without doubt the most notable and the best preserved of the three still standing in the port area. The caravansary is a type of structure found throughout the entire Eastern world: in practice it is a sort of primitive inn which in the past provided accommodations for the caravans, pilgrims and merchants and offered them refreshment and rest, and a respite from their long and extenuating journeys. Built in the second half of the 18th Century, this Khan is famous for its spacious courtyard surrounded by a charming two-tier portico. The lower tier features an elegant arcade of pointed arches leaping from capitals supported by pillars, a feature explaining the name of the building. At the center of the courtyard is an interesting octagonal well. The gracious tower rising from the building is an architectural element of evident Islamic inspiration added on in 1906, still known as the **Clock Tower** despite the fact that the timepiece has been removed.

44

Saint John of Acre, an image of the Church of St. John and vistas of the picturesque port surrounded by monumental buildings.

Saint John of Acre, a view of the seawalls; in the background the Church of St. John.

THE OLD PORT

The appearance of today's port, while impressive, does not do justice to the importance of the Saint John of Acre landing in ancient times, when it was a principal stopover along important strategic and commercial sea routes. In Crusader times the Republics of Genoa, Pisa and Venice each had their own docks, storehouses and emporiums there. Today the port is partially silted up and is now a harbour for fishing boats and pleasure craft.

REMAINS OF THE ANCIENT WALLS

Only a very small portion of the mighty walled bastions that still today circle the city date to the time of the Crusades. The greater part, built by Daher-el-Amar and reinforced by Ahmed el Jazzar, dates to the second half of the 18th Century. The walls were partly restored after a naval bombardment in 1840.

Saint John of Acre, these beautiful images document the local color and atmosphere of the ancient port area of the Crusader city. Today the port offers a safe haven for fishing boats as well as for pleasure craft.
The oldest circle of walls runs all around the port area, while here and there are discernible some of the most interesting monuments in Akko: for example, the Clock Tower rising above the Caravansary of the Pillars, the dome and the pointed minaret of the Sinan Pasha Mosque, and stretches of seawalls, with the bell-tower of the Church of St. John in the background. Ancient ruins also emerge from the rippled surface of the sea.

CHURCH OF SAINT JOHN

This place of worship, with its small cupola and simple bell-tower, hugs the solid bastions of the sea walls, not far from the **Lighthouse**, on the jutting point of the promontory. The Church of St. John was built by the Franciscan monks during the first half of the 17th Century.

MUSEUM OF HEROISM

The Museum of Heroism occupies a portion of the Citadel, which has been partially converted for use as a psychiatric hospital. Open to the public are the various chambers destined for incarceration, among which the cell occupied by Bahaullah, as well as the sinister *Gallows Room* in which the macabre implement used for execution of the Jewish rebels against the British mandate is displayed. Of note the *terrace* of the Citadel, which offers a spellbinding panorama of the historical center of the city and of the coastline.

Saint John of Acre (Museum of Heroism), these images document some aspects of the museum, situated inside the Citadel, of which the side leading into the prisons is shown. Besides the cells and the Gallows Room, with its eternal flame, the visitor will also see, on one wall, illustrations of one of the dramatic attempts by Jewish underground members to break into the fortress and free their comrades.

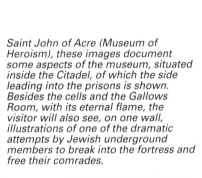

Caesarea, a bird's eye view of the port area

CAESAREA

Only in relatively recent times have archaeological surveys and the first excavations made it possible for tourists and visitors to admire that which is universally considered the most representative of Israel's archaeological sites.

The ancient ruins, the walls, the columns and the awesome remains of that which was the most important Roman colony in the territory of the modern-day Hebrew state lie in an inspiring setting near the coast in the upper portion of what is called the Sharon Plain. Long ago it was the site of a colony known as *Tower of Strato* (4th Century B.C.), founded by the Phoenicians, precursors of the Hellenic and Roman civilizations, as a stopover for commercial traffic along the sea routes for Lebanon and Egypt. In 22 B.C., Herod the Great founded a city on the site and named it *Caesarea* in honor of the Emperor Augustus (*Caesar*). Proclaimed the residence of the governor of Judea in 6 B.C., the city became the most important Roman administrative center in Palestine. Among Caesarea's illustrious visitors and residents number Pontius Pilate and the apostle Paul, who was imprisoned there for two years. In 66 A.D., the first revolts against Roman rule sparked the first of the Jewish wars and the harsh Roman repression that followed. In 69 A.D. Vespasian was crowned Emperor in Caesarea, and bestowed on the city the title of *Colonia Prima Flavia Augusta Caesarea*. Although Caesarea gained renown as a center of first Hellenistic and later Christian culture, it also had its share of martyrs, among whom the Hebrew philosopher and the-

orist Rabbi Akiva, killed there in 135 A.D. In the 4th Century, the theologian Eusebius became the Bishop of Caesarea. In 1101, Baldwin I captured and held the city under the Crusader banner; it was during this period that the *Holy Grail*, or 'Sacred Basin' identified by tradition with the chalice used by Christ at the Last Supper, was conveyed from Caesarea to the Cathedral of San Lorenzo in Genoa. Despite the fact that Caesarea was, in 1254, retaken by Louis IX of France, who fortified it with new defences, the city fell once and for all to the Muslims later in the 13th Century and its irreversible decline began.

Caesarea, the suggestive interior of the East Gate and its entryway opening through the Byzantine wall.

Caesarea, these views show the ruins of ancient Crusader buildings, portions of the walls, and the characteristic ogival arches.

Caesarea, among the most ancient remains are the ruins of the Temple of Augustus.

Caesarea, more images from the fascinating archaeological site, with its ruins spanning time from the age of ancient Rome through the period of the Crusades.

Caesarea, these views show the port area, with its bathing beach and ruins emerging from the waters of the sea. Long ago this was the site of a settlement of Muslim refugees from Bosnia. Of the coastal village, later abandoned, there remain today the ancient buildings and the Mosque with its minaret.

EAST GATE

The Roman city, during its period of maximum splendour, extended far beyond the area covered by the Caesarea of the Crusaders. The East Gate, leading into the old Crusader city, opens in the Byzantine circle of walls. A powerful ogival arch breaching the massive stone barrier dominates the exterior, while the gatehouse enclosure itself, with its stone flooring shadowed by a vaulted ceiling with ribbed transepts, is permeated by the atmosphere of times past.

These stylistic touches, typical of the Gothic architectures, stand mute testimony to how the influence of the Gothic style had spread, in the wake of the Crusaders, to even the most remote corners of the Southeastern portion of the Mediterranean basin.

A VISIT TO THE EXCAVATIONS

Caesarea's awe-inspiring archaeological site, in which excavations began in the 1960s, contains a unique medley of ruins that date from the Roman age through Crusader times. Among the Roman remains within the medieval city walls are those of the **Temple of Augustus**, erected under Herod. The Crusader ruins are for the most part vestiges of streets and walls, and an ample profusion of ogival arches.

THE PORT AREA

The remains of constructions, and ruins reaching all the way down to the sea, are still visible near the ancient port of Caesarea. Centuries of neglect, and earthquakes, have cancelled the oldest evidence (dating to the Roman period), but vestiges of the Crusader fortifications still stand.

Particularly memorable among these is the **Citadel**, flanked by the defensive works of the port. The port itself is today used mainly by fishermen; nearby the visitor will also find a pleasant sandy beach with refreshment stands.

The unmistakable outline of a **Mosque**, watched over by its sharply-pointed minaret, is the only reminder of the fishing village, that once stood here founded in the second half of the nineteenth century by a community of Bosnian Muslims and later abandoned following a malaria epidemic.

Caesarea, a view of the Byzantine road with its Roman statues, and a detail of the headless sculptures in red porphyry.
Caesarea, two views of the grandiose Roman Amphitheatre, after restoration.

BYZANTINE ROAD

It is quite likely that the so-called 'Byzantine Road', or the *Avenue of the Statues*, identifies the site once occupied by the Roman Forum. Discovered at the beginning of the 1950s by the inhabitants of the nearby **Kibbutz Sdot Yam**, the site has yielded up two valuable expressions of Roman statuary art, housed in a Byzantine building dating to the 5th-6th Century.The statues are two headless seated figures, one in marble and one in red porphyry. The latter, in a solemn pose on a grey porphyry seat, is most probably an *Emperor* or an *Imperial Dignitary* (2nd-3rd Centuries A.D.).

ROMAN AMPHITHEATRE

Caesarea's amphitheatre, showing a remarkable affinity with that of Beit Shean, is among the most imposing expressions of Roman architecture to be found in the East. Located a short distance from the sea, in a delightfully evocative setting, it has been restored to its ancient splendour thanks to the extensive restoration work led by expert Italian archaeologists (beginning at the end of the 1950s). The *Cavea* built during Herod's time, has even today lost none of its impressiveness. Performances are held during the summer months.

Caesarea, sunset over the ancient Roman Aqueduct.

A view of the golf course at the Dan Caesarea Golf facilities.

ROMAN AQUEDUCT

The majestic remains of an aqueduct dating to the Roman period extend for about nine kilometers to the north of the Crusader city. The stonework, today partially concealed by the shoreline dunes, dates to the 2nd Century A.D.

DAN CAESAREA GOLF COURSE

The outskirts of Caesarea are densely built up, and offer a wealth of accommodations for tourists. Among these, the excellent facilities of the golf course adjacent to the luxurious and polished Dan Caesarea Hotel merit special mention.

BEIT SHEARIM

The Beit Shearim archaeological site, one of Israel's most interesting, is situated in Galilee, halfway along the route from Haifa to Nazareth. In ancient times it was a Maccabee settlement, and was later to become a leading center for the spread of Hebrew culture and religion when the *Mishnah* (compendium of Hebrew doctrine and theory based on Old Testament principles) was codified by Rabbi Yehuda Hanassi in the 2nd Century A.D.. In a later period the city was destroyed and reduced to a pile of ruins by the Romans.

The vast underground **Necropolis** excavated in the hillside is particularly fascinating, with its many tombs discovered in a conspicuous number of burial chambers. Even should the traditional belief (as yet with no proven foundation) that many were tombs reserved for the exponents of the local Synedrion and for Rabbi Hanassi himself find confirmation, the sheer number of sarcophagi contained in the necropolis is no less astounding. An explanation may lie in the by now established fact that after the Roman prohibition on the Hebrews' burying their dead at the Mount of Olives in Jerusalem, the custom of transferring the dead to this city in Galilee, believed to be 'holy', became more deep-rooted than ever. The sarcophagi are adorned with numerous inscriptions in Greek, Hebrew and Aramaic characters, and with symbols attesting to their Hebrew and pagan origins: proof that the corpses that rest at Beit Shearim are of the most diversified provenance, certainly, but also of the evident placement of the sarcophagi in the context of that classical art that came to its maturity in this ancient center of Hebrew culture and tradition.

Beit Shearim, a general view and the entry to the ipogean catacombs.

Beit Shearim, these images show the interiors of the burial chambers with the sarcophagi.

Following page: *Beit Shearim, the ruins of the Synagogue and the Hebrew symbols sculpted in the rock.*

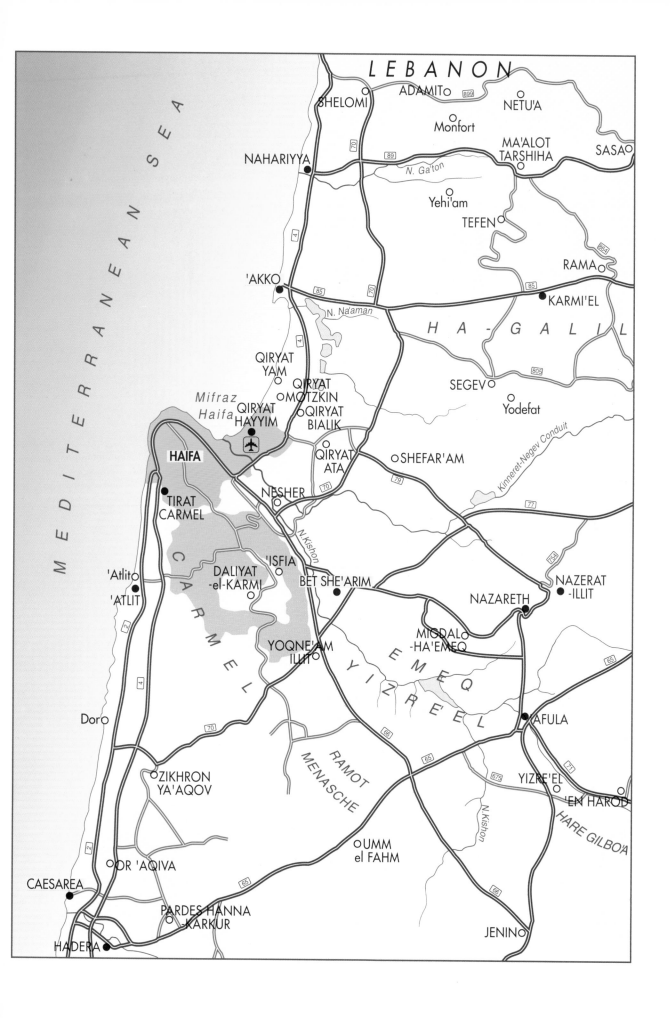

INDEX

© Copyright 1994 by Casa Editrice Bonechi, via Cairoli 18/b - 50131 Florence - Italy
Tel. 55/576841 - Telex 571323 CEB - Fax 55/5000766
All rights reserved. No part of this book may be reproduced without the written permission of the Publisher.
Printed in Italy by Centro Stampa Editoriale Bonechi
Text: Giuliano Valdes - Editing Studio, Pisa
Translation: Paula Boomsliter for TRADUCO s.n.c., Florence

Photographs from the archives of Casa Editrice Bonechi taken by Paolo Giambone *except those*
taken by Andrea Pistolesi *on pages:* 30, 31 bottom, 36, 37 bottom left, 38, 39, 41 bottom, 43, 44, 45, 58, 59 top.
Photographs on pages 28 center left, 31 top, 49 *were kindly provided by Albatross Aerial Photography, Tel Aviv.*
The Publishers are grateful to the Mane Katz Museum in Haifa for the kind collaboration.
Map: Studio Grafico Bellandi & Mariani, Pistoia

ISBN 88-8029-124-6

* * *